RAYMOND BUCKLAND'S

ALCHEMY COLORING BOOK

QVP

Queen Victoria Press

RAYMOND BUCKLAND'S ALCHEMY COLORING BOOK

Copyright © 2017 Raymond Buckland

Illustrations by Raymond Buckland

ISBN 978-0-9978481-7-5

Queen Victoria Press
153 E. South Street, Ste. 892
Wooster, OH 55691-0892

The full-color, 50 card deck, The Cards of
Alchemy, is available directly from
Queen Victoria Press, P.O. Box 892, Wooster,
OH 44691-0892
It is also featured for sale at eBay.com
$28 per deck, post paid in the U.S.

Introduction to Alchemy

Alchemy is the art or science by which the chemical philosophers of old attempted to transmute base metals into precious metals. There were actually three main quests. One was the change from base metals into silver or gold, but additionally there was a search for a universal solvent (*menstruum universale*) of enormous potency that would not only transform metals but would also have powers of healing and of perfecting things. A third goal was discovery of an elixir of life; a fountain of perpetual youth.

The ancient art of alchemy led to today's chemistry. The first laboratories were alchemical laboratories. All chemical apparatus used up until the beginning of the eighteenth century was actually invented by alchemists, who were the first to practice distillation and sublimation.

Early alchemical texts were hand-written and many used their own form of shorthand when describing procedures. Some of the symbolism was also used to keep a particular alchemist's discoveries secret from others.

The apparatus is usually well described, often with clear illustrations, but the nature of the substances used and the methods employed can be quite obscure to the present-day seeker.

The early basic symbolism uses the sun to represent gold and the moon for silver. Copper is given the (astrological) sign of Venus, lead the sign of Saturn, iron for Mars, and tin for Hermes. However, later Mercury was mercury and Jupiter was tin. There were more complex representations for alloys. For example, electrum (a combination of gold and silver) was represented by the sun and the moon conjoined; The sun with a single ray coming from it was pure gold but with two rays was chrysocolla (solder of gold).

Some of the other symbolism: a stag was the soul; a unicorn the spirit; a green lion was acid; a serpent (or a snake or dragon) represented the matter in its imperfect, unregenerate state; volatilization was shown in the form of birds taking flight.

Raymond Buckland has produced a set of (colored) cards – much like tarot cards – that can be used for personal transformation and spiritual development. The black-and-white illustrations in this present book are taken from those cards. There is also a complete book titled *The Book of Alchemy.*

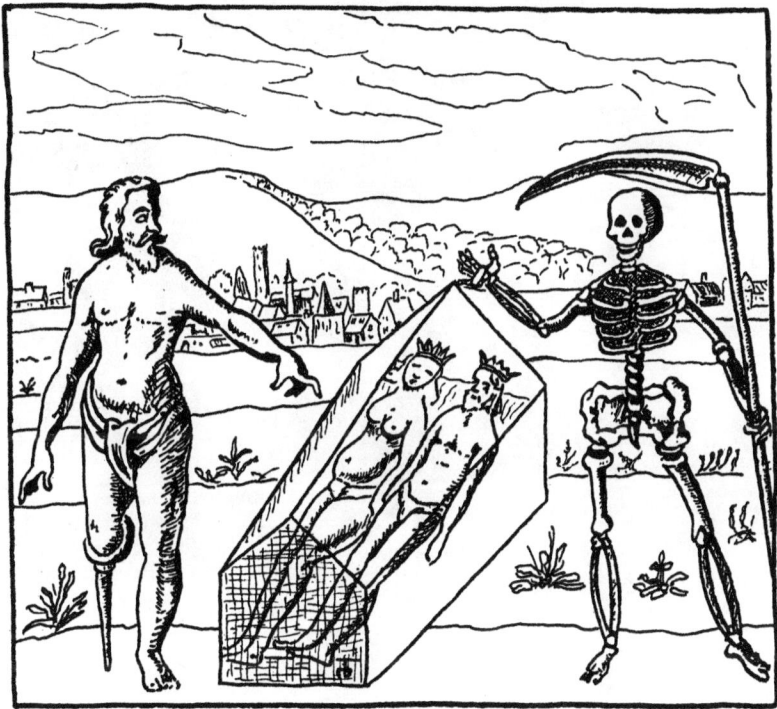

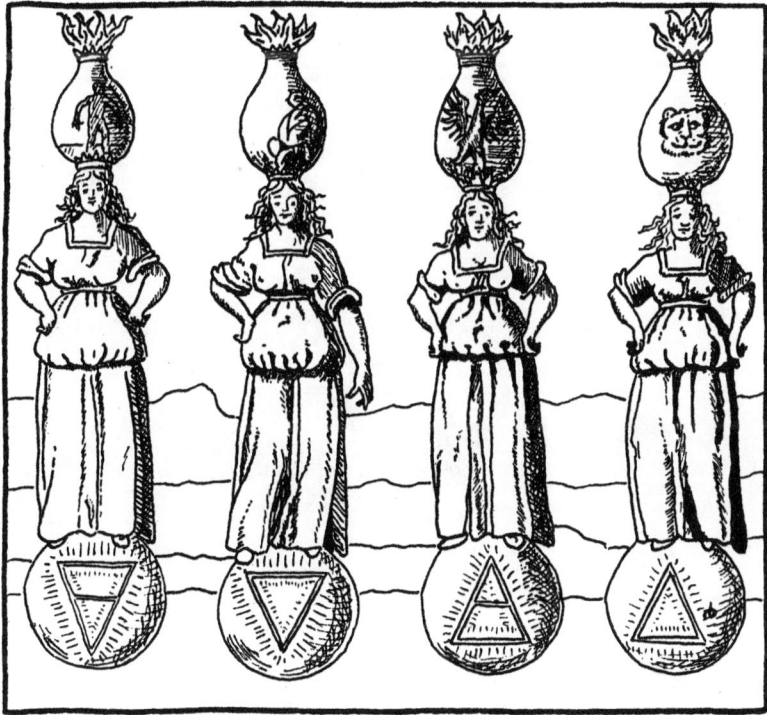

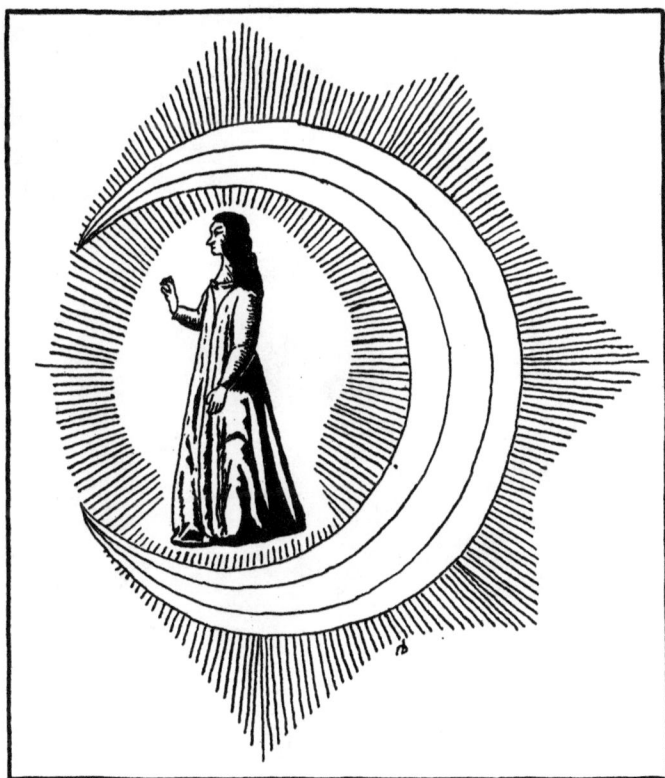

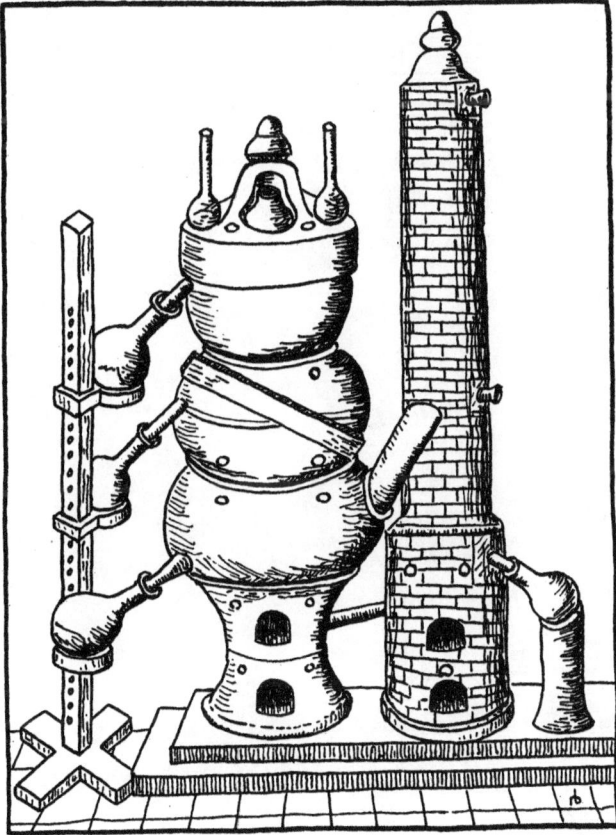

QUEEN VICTORIA PRESS

Fiction by Raymond Buckland

A MISTAKE THROUGH THE HEART - Book Three of the
   Bram Stoker mysteries (Books One and Two were
   published by Penguin/Random House's Berkley Prime
   Crime imprint)
CHURCHILL'S SECRET SPY - WWII espionage novel
THE PENNY COURT ENQUIRERS - Victorian mystery series
   ONE CLUE AT A TIME   Book One
   THE NOBLE SAVAGE   Book Two
   DEADLY SPIRIT Book Three
OUT OF THIS WORLD - Science fiction short story collection
PARANORMAL POETRY - Poetry, strange and unusual
LAFF WITH OLAF - A mixed bag of cartoons
In preparation:
   THE WIITIKO INHERITANCE
   THE SECRET LIFE OF MISS EMMELINE CROMWELL

Non-fiction by Raymond Buckland

WITCHCRAFT REVEALED - An examination of Witchcraft
   and Wicca
OUIJA CONNECTION TO SPIRIT - The Talking Board and
   how to contact the Spirit World
PARANORMAL PRIMER - "How-to" on many popular meta-
   physical practices
HERE IS THE OCCULT - An introduction to the wide world
   of the paranormal
RAYMOND BUCKLAND'S ALCHEMY COLORING BOOK
In preparation:
   THE BOOK OF ALCHEMY
   PSYCHIC WORLD SECRETS
   ANATOMY OF THE PARANORMAL

Fiction by Eileen Lizzie Wells

FLETCHER'S FOLLY - A Gothic romance mystery
In preparation:
THE POSTMISTRESS MYSTERIES
DESIGNING WOMEN

www.ingramcontent.com/pod-product-compliance
Lightning Source LLC
Chambersburg PA
CBHW061754020426
42331CB00006B/1479